T he Australian Women's Weekly's *Italian Cooking Class Cookbook* was first published in 1981 and has been reprinted 9 times. It has sold more than one million copies worldwide and established itself as a genuine international classic, to this day still in print and still finding new and enthusiastic fans.

●

It contains more than 100 recipes, most of them illustrated with step-by-step photography.

●

This Home Library *Mini Classic* is intended to introduce you to this acclaimed cookbook. We have selected more than 60 firm favourites for you to try your hand at, to allow you sample Italian cuisine at its most enticing.

Produced by The Australian Women's Weekly Home Library.
Typeset by ACP Colour Graphics Pty Ltd. Colour separations by Times Printers Pte Ltd, Singapore.
Printing by Offset Alpine Printing Limited, Sydney. Published by ACP Publishing Pty Limited, 54 Park Street, Sydney.
♦ AUSTRALIA: Distributed by Network Distribution Company, 54 Park Street Sydney, (02) 282 8777.
♦ UNITED KINGDOM: Distributed in the U.K. by Australian Consolidated Press (UK) Ltd, 20 Galowhill Rd, Brackmills, Northampton NN4 7EE (01604) 760 456.
♦ CANADA: Distributed in Canada by Whitecap Books Ltd, 351 Lynn Ave, North Vancouver B.C. V7P 3J6 (604) 980 9852.
♦ NEW ZEALAND: Distributed in New Zealand by Netlink Distribution Company, 17B Hargreaves St, Level 3, College Hill, Auckland 1 (9) 302 7616.
♦ SOUTH AFRICA: Distributed in South Africa by Intermag, PO Box 57394, Springfield 2137 (011) 493 3200.

© A C P Publishing Pty Limited 1995
ACN 053 273 546
This publication is copyright. No part of it may be reproduced or transmitted in any form without the written permission of the publishers.

BRITISH & NORTH AMERICAN READERS: Please note that Australian cup and spoon measurements are metric. A quick conversion guide appears on page 64.

ANTIPASTO

Antipasto makes a light and tempting start to a meal.

Eggplant Appetiser

Recipe can be made 2 days ahead. Serve hot or cold. Not suitable to freeze.

- 2 large eggplants
- 1 cup olive oil
- ¼ cup olive oil, extra
- 3 cloves garlic, crushed
- 3 ripe tomatoes, peeled, seeded, chopped
- 1 tablespoon tomato paste
- ½ cup water

Cut washed, unpeeled eggplants lenthwise into 5mm slices. Cut slices into 6cm lengths.

Heat oil in pan, add half the eggplants, cook, stirring gently, about 5 minutes or until eggplants are soft. Remove from pan with slotted spoon. Repeat with remaining eggplants.

Heat extra oil in frying pan, add garlic, tomatoes, paste and water. Simmer, uncovered, about 10 minutes or until sauce is thick. Add eggplants, stir lightly to combine.

Marinated Mushrooms

Recipe can be made 2 days ahead. Not suitable to freeze.

250g button mushrooms
¼ cup lemon juice
½ cup olive oil
2 tablespoons chopped fresh parsley
¼ teaspoon dried tarragon leaves
¼ teaspoon ground black pepper

Wash mushrooms, remove stalks, slice mushrooms thinly.

Combine juice, oil, parsley, tarragon and pepper in bowl. Mix well. Add mushrooms; mix well. Cover. Refrigerate 4 hours or overnight.

Marinated mushrooms are also delicious tossed into a green salad. Remove mushrooms from marinade with slotted spoon, add to salad greens; add enough of the marinade to coat salad greens lightly; toss well.

Beans with Tomato

Recipe can be made a day ahead. Reheat just before serving. Not suitable to freeze. Canned borlotti or cannellini beans (300g) can be substituted for Continental beans. Drain and rinse beans, add for last 10 minutes of cooking.

1kg Continental beans
2 onions
3 ripe tomatoes
45g can anchovy fillets
30g butter
1 clove garlic, crushed
1½ tablespoons tomato paste
1 teaspoon dried basil leaves
½ teaspoon sugar
1 cup water

Shell beans, discard pods. Finely chop onions. Peel and chop tomatoes. Drain and finely chop anchovies.

Melt butter in pan, add garlic, onions, tomatoes and anchovies, cook, stirring, until onion is soft. Stir in beans, paste, basil, sugar and water. Simmer, covered, about 30 minutes or until beans are tender.

Sicilian Caponata

Recipe can be made a day ahead. Reheat just before serving. Not suitable to freeze. This dish also makes an excellent vegetable accompaniment to main courses.

1 eggplant
salt
¼ cup olive oil
1 onion, chopped
2 red peppers, chopped
1 stick celery, sliced
400g can peeled tomatoes
2 tablespoons brown vinegar
1 tablespoon sugar
1 clove garlic, crushed
8 seedless black olives, sliced
1 tablespoon drained capers

Cut eggplant into 1cm cubes, place in colander, sprinkle with salt, stand 1 hour. Rinse well, pat dry with absorbent paper. Heat oil in large pan, add onion, peppers and celery, cook, stirring, 5 minutes.

Add eggplant, cook, stirring, further 5 minutes. Sieve undrained tomatoes into pan, discard seeds.

Add vinegar, sugar and garlic, cook, stirring, further 2 minutes. Stir in olives and capers, simmer, uncovered, about 15 minutes or until most of the liquid has been evaporated.

Pepper Relish

Recipe can be made 3 days ahead. Serve cold. Not suitable to freeze.

3 green peppers
3 onions
3 ripe tomatoes
2 tablespoons olive oil
½ cup white vinegar

Remove seeds from peppers, slice peppers lengthways. Peel and slice onions. Peel and chop tomatoes.

Place peppers, onions, tomatoes and oil in large pan, simmer, covered, 1 hour, stirring occasionally.

Add vinegar, simmer, uncovered, 15 minutes. Place in bowl or in jar, cover; refrigerate until cold.

Glazed Onions

Recipe can be made 2 days ahead. Serve hot or cold. Not suitable to freeze.

500g small pickling onions
¼ cup olive oil
¼ white vinegar
1½ tablespoons sugar
4 whole cloves
1 bay leaf

Place unpeeled onions in bowl, cover with boiling water, stand 5 minutes.

Drain onions. Using a small sharp knife, peel onions, taking care to leave ends intact so onions do not fall apart during cooking.

Combine oil, vinegar, sugar, cloves and bay leaf in pan. Add onions, simmer gently, covered, about 20 minutes or until onions are tender and sauce turns syrupy.

Crostini

Crostini rounds and mushroom topping can be made a day ahead. Assemble crostini just before baking. Crostini rounds suitable to freeze.

12 slices white bread
30g butter, melted
45g butter, extra
2 tablespoons plain flour
1 cup milk
¼ cup grated parmesan cheese
90g mushrooms, finely chopped
2 teaspoons anchovy paste
2 tablespoons grated parmesan cheese, extra
50g can rolled fillets of anchovies, drained
3 seedless black olives, sliced
3 seedless green olives, sliced
¼ red or green pepper, thinly sliced

Cut 5cm rounds of bread using cutter, brush with butter, place on oven tray. Bake in moderate oven about 10 minutes or until golden brown; cool.

Melt extra butter in pan, add flour, cook, stirring, 1 minute. Remove from heat, gradually add milk, stir over heat until mixture boils and thickens; remove from heat. Add cheese, mushrooms and paste; mix well.

Spread 2 teaspoons of mixture over each bread round, top with extra cheese. Top with anchovies, olives or pepper strips. Bake in hot oven about 5 minutes or until lightly browned and heated through.

Makes about 24.

SOUPS

Italian soups can be clear and light or thick and hearty, but they are always full of flavour.

Minestrone

Recipe can be made 2 days ahead. Reheat just before serving. Not suitable to freeze. Grated parmesan cheese can be served with minestrone, if desired.

3 carrots
3 sticks celery
2 onions
250g potatoes
2 zucchini
90g green beans
½ cup olive oil
45g butter
250g cabbage, shredded
1.25 litres (5 cups) beef stock
2 x 400g cans peeled whole tomatoes
310g can cannellini beans

Finely chop carrots, celery, onions, potatoes, zucchini and beans. Heat oil and butter in large pan, add onions, cook, stirring, until pale golden brown. Add carrots, cook, stirring, about 3 minutes or until almost tender.

Repeat cooking with potatoes, then celery, zucchini, beans and cabbage. Stir in stock and undrained crushed tomatoes. Simmer, covered, 1½ hours. Stir in rinsed and drained beans, simmer, covered, further 15 minutes or until soup is thick.
Serves 4 to 6.

Stracciatella

Stock can be made 4 days ahead. Soup best made just before serving. Stock suitable to freeze.

2 chicken thighs, skinned
1 carrot, chopped
1 onion, chopped
1 stick celery, chopped
1.5 litres (6 cups) water
1 teaspoon black peppercorns
2 eggs
60g grated parmesan cheese
¼ cup chopped
   fresh parsley
ground black pepper

Place chicken, vegetables, water and peppercorns in large pan, simmer, covered, 1 hour.

Strain stock through sieve into another pan. Discard chicken and vegetables; only the chicken stock is required in this soup. (Chicken and vegetables can be used for another meal.) Skim a clean piece of absorbent paper over surface of hot stock to remove any fat. Repeat two or three times, using fresh paper. (Alternatively, cool broth, refrigerate until cold; remove fat from surface.)

Beat eggs, cheese and parsley together in jug or bowl. Bring stock to boil in pan. While stirring vigorously with one hand, add egg mixture gradually in a thin stream with the other. Continue stirring over heat 1 to 2 minutes after all egg mixture has been added; remove mixture from heat immediately. Season with pepper.

Serves 4 to 6.

Meatball Soup

Stock can be made 4 days ahead. Meatballs can be made a day ahead. Soup best made just before serving. Stock and meatballs suitable to freeze.

750g beef bones
2 carrots
2 sticks celery
400g can peeled tomatoes
½ cup small pasta
1 tablespoon chopped fresh parsley
MEATBALLS
500g minced beef
1 egg
½ cup fresh breadcrumbs

Place beef bones, carrots and celery in large pan, cover with cold water, simmer, covered, 1 hour. Skim any fat from soup while it is cooking.

Remove celery and carrots from stock, cool; chop. Remove bones from stock, strain stock into large bowl; return to pan. Add carrots, celery and undrained crushed tomatoes, simmer, covered, 15 minutes.

Add pasta to pan of boiling water, boil, uncovered, until just tender; drain. Add pasta to soup with meatballs, simmer further 10 minutes; stir in parsley.

Meatballs: Combine beef, egg and breadcrumbs in bowl; mix well. Roll heaped teaspoons of mixture into balls. Place in small greased baking dish in single layer. Bake meatballs, covered, in moderate oven 45 minutes, turning occasionally. Remove, drain on absorbent paper.

Serves 6.

Baccala Soup

Baccala is dried, salted cod. Recipe can be made a day ahead. Reheat just before serving. Not suitable to freeze.

450g packet baccala fillets
¼ cup olive oil
2 cloves garlic, crushed
2 onions, thinly sliced
1 stick celery, finely chopped
¼ teaspoon dried thyme leaves
1 tablespoon chopped fresh parsley
400g can peeled tomatoes
¼ cup dry white wine
1 litre (4 cups) water
2 potatoes, chopped
1 tablespoon chopped fresh parsley, extra
¼ teaspoon ground black pepper

Soak baccala in large bowl of water for 36 hours, changing water frequently. Drain well, dry thoroughly with absorbent paper. Cut baccala into pieces, removing as many bones and as much skin as possible (or remove during cooking time).

Heat oil in large pan, add garlic and onions, cook, stirring, over low heat until golden but not browned. Add celery, thyme and parsley, cook, stirring, 3 minutes.

Sieve undrained tomatoes into pan; discard seeds. Simmer, covered, 10 minutes. Add wine, water and potatoes to pan. Add baccala, simmer gently, uncovered, 1 hour. Stir in extra parsley and pepper.
Serves 4.

Mussel Soup

Recipe best made close to serving. Stock can be made several hours ahead. Stock suitable to freeze.

24 mussels
500g white fish fillets
1.5 litres (6 cups) water
1 stick celery, chopped
1 onion, chopped
1 carrot, chopped
30g butter
¼ cup plain flour
2 teaspoons curry powder
2 tablespoons tomato paste
2 chicken stock cubes
2 tomatoes, peeled, chopped
ground black pepper
2 tablespoons chopped fresh parsley

Clean mussels by scrubbing them with a brush under cold running water. Remove beard – the hairy substance around each – by pulling.

Skin and bone fish, cut fish into large portions. Combine fish, water and vegetables in large pan, simmer, covered, 15 minutes.

Drain mixture, reserve stock and fish; discard vegetables. Melt butter in pan, add flour and curry powder, cook, stirring, 1 minute. Remove from heat, gradually add combined paste and fish stock. Stir over heat until soup boils and thickens. Add crumbled stock cubes, tomatoes and pepper; simmer 1 minute.

Add mussels and flaked fish, simmer further 5 minutes or until mussels have opened. Stir in chopped parsley. Serves 6.

Fish Soup

Recipe best made close to serving. Stock can be made 6 hours ahead. Stock suitable to freeze.

4 red fish fillets
2 onions, sliced
few sprigs fresh parsley
1 stick celery, chopped
1.25 litres (5 cups) water
1 cup dry white wine
250g cooked prawns
250g mussels
250g pipis
400g can whole tomatoes
500g fish fillets, extra
2 ripe tomatoes, peeled, seeded, chopped
2 potatoes, chopped
1 clove garlic, crushed
1 teaspoon dried oregano leaves
½ teaspoon sugar
1 tablespoon tomato paste
¼ ground black pepper
2 tablespoons chopped fresh parsley

Combine the 4 fish fillets, onions, parsley, celery, water and wine in large pan, simmer, covered, 30 minutes. Strain stock through fine sieve, return stock to pan, discard vegetables. Flake fish and reserve.

Shell and devein prawns. Scrub mussels; remove beards. Scrub pipis. Place mussels and pipis in large pan of boiling water, boil, covered, until shells open; remove immediately from water.

Sieve undrained canned tomatoes; discard seeds. Remove skin and any bones from extra fish, chop fish. Add canned and chopped tomatoes, fish, potatoes, garlic, oregano, sugar, paste and pepper to stock. Simmer, covered, further 30 minutes. Add prawns and reserved fish to soup, bring to boil, add parsley, mussels and pipis, simmer until heated through.

Serves 6.

Brodo

Recipe can be made 3 days ahead. Suitable to freeze. Ask your butcher to slice the veal shank for you. If you want a good, hearty soup, the meat and chicken can be returned to the soup with chopped parsley. Cooked tortellini, cooked pasta or thinly sliced cooked vegetables can also be added.

500g boned beef shank
1 carrot
2 chicken thighs, skinned
1 stick celery, chopped
1 onion, quartered
1 small potato, peeled
½ green pepper, chopped
1 veal shank, sliced

Remove any excess fat from beef and chicken. Cut beef into small pieces. Quarter carrot lengthways. Combine all ingredients in large pan, add cold water to cover. Cook, partially covered, over high heat until boiling. Simmer, covered, skimming foam from surface frequently, 3 hours.

Remove beef, chicken and veal; reserve for another meal. Strain stock through large strainer lined with cheesecloth or clean tea-towel; discard vegetable mixture. Cool, cover, refrigerate several hours or overnight; remove fat from stock. Bring stock to boil just before serving.

Makes about 4 cups.

Lentil Soup

Recipe can be made 2 days ahead. Reheat just before serving. Suitable to freeze. Bacon bones are very salty, so there is no need to add extra salt to this recipe.

15g butter
1 tablespoon olive oil
1 onion, chopped
1 carrot, chopped
1 stick celery, chopped
250g bacon bones
250g brown lentils
400g can tomatoes
1 litre (4 cups) water
2 beef stock cubes
¼ teaspoon ground black pepper
2 tablespoons chopped fresh parsley

Heat butter and oil in pan, add onion, carrot and celery, cook, stirring, until onion is soft. Add bacon bones, lentils, undrained crushed tomatoes, water and crumbled stock cubes. Simmer, covered, about 1½ hours or until lentils are tender. Remove and discard bacon bones; add pepper and parsley.

Serves 4.

SAUCES FOR PASTA

Spoon these sauces over any favourite pasta: spaghetti, fettuccine, tagliatelle, macaroni, etc.

Siciliana

Recipe can be made a day ahead. Reheat just before serving. Not suitable to freeze.

1 small eggplant
1 small green pepper
45g can anchovy fillets
milk
10 seedless black olives
1 tablespoon capers
⅓ cup olive oil
1 onion, grated
2 cloves garlic, crushed
2 x 400g cans whole tomatoes
½ teaspoon dried basil (or 1 teaspoon chopped fresh basil)
¼ cup chopped parsley
¼ teaspoon ground black pepper

Peel and chop eggplant; chop pepper. Drain anchovies, cover with milk in bowl, stand 10 minutes; drain anchovies well (this removes excess salt). Finely chop anchovies, olives and capers.

Heat oil in pan, add eggplant, pepper and onion, cook, stirring, until eggplant is soft. Add garlic, undrained crushed tomatoes and basil, simmer, covered, 30 minutes. Add anchovies, olives, capers, parsley and black pepper, simmer, covered, further 5 minutes.

Serves 4 to 6.

Seafood

Recipe best made just before serving. Not suitable to freeze.

125g scallops
500g cooked prawns
60g butter
2 cloves garlic, crushed
½ cup dry white wine
300ml carton cream
1 tablespoon arrowroot or cornflour
¼ cup water
1 teaspoon lemon juice
1 tablespoon chopped fresh parsley
3 green shallots, chopped
8 oysters in half shells

Clean scallops and separate coral; cut scallops in half. Shell, devein and coarsely chop prawns.

Melt butter in pan, add garlic, cook, stirring, until fragrant. Add wine and cream, bring to boil, boil, uncovered, 4 minutes. Stir in blended arrowroot and water, stir until mixture boils. Add scallops, prawns and juice, simmer 2 minutes or until scallops are just cooked. Stir in parsley and shallots. Garnish with oysters drizzled with a little sauce.

Serves 4.

Pesto

Recipe can be made a week ahead. Spoon into jar, cover pesto with olive oil, top with lid; keep refrigerated. Suitable to freeze without cheese.

3 bunches fresh basil
1 tablespoon olive oil
2 tablespoons pine nuts
2 cloves garlic, crushed
ground black pepper
¼ cup olive oil, extra
¼ cup grated parmesan cheese

Wash basil, remove leaves from stems, discard stems. (You will need about 2 cups of leaves.) Combine oil and pine nuts in small pan, cook, stirring, over low heat until pine nuts are lightly browned; drain immediately.

Process basil, pine nuts, garlic and pepper until finely chopped and smooth. With motor operating, add extra oil in a thin stream. Process further 1 second. (Blender can also be used; stop blender and scrape down mixture occasionally.) Transfer mixture to bowl, add cheese; mix well.
Serves 4 to 6.

Pescatore

Recipe best made just before serving. Not suitable to freeze.

500g mussels
90g crab meat
2 ripe tomatoes, peeled
½ green pepper
500g fish fillets
2 x 400g cans whole tomatoes
2 tablespoons olive oil
¼ cup dry white wine

Scrub mussels, remove beards. Add mussels to pan of boiling water, boil about 3 minutes or until mussels open; drain. Remove mussels from shells.

Flake crab. Chop ripe tomatoes; finely chop pepper. Skin and bone fish, cut into 1cm pieces. Sieve undrained canned tomatoes into bowl; discard seeds.

Heat oil in pan, add fish, cook, stirring gently, until lightly browned. Add chopped tomato, pepper, sieved tomatoes and wine, simmer, uncovered, 10 minutes, stirring occasionally. Add crabmeat and mussels, simmer until sauce is heated through.

Serves 6.

Chicken Livers

Recipe best made just before serving. Not suitable to freeze.

**250g chicken livers
¼ cup olive oil
2 onions, chopped
⅔ cup cream
2 eggs, lightly beaten
grated parmesan cheese**

Wash, trim and chop livers. Heat oil in pan, add onions, cook, stirring, until lightly browned. Add livers, cook until they just change colour.

Add cream; mix well. Simmer, uncovered, 2 minutes. Quickly stir in eggs; remove from heat immediately. Serve topped with parmesan cheese. Serves 2.

Marinara

Recipe best made just before serving. Not suitable to freeze.

500g prawns
250g scallops
45g can flat anchovy fillets
8 oysters
½ cup water
½ cup dry white wine
2 tablespoons olive oil
5 large ripe tomatoes, peeled, chopped
2 cloves garlic, crushed
1 tablespoon tomato paste
1 tablespoon chopped fresh parsley
1 tablespoon chopped fresh mint
ground black pepper

Shell and devein prawns; cut scallops in half. Drain anchovies on absorbent paper; chop finely. Carefully remove oysters from shells.

Combine water and wine in frying pan, add scallops, cook 1 minute; drain, remove from pan. Heat oil in pan, add tomatoes, garlic and paste, stir until combined, simmer, uncovered, 2 minutes. Add seafood, simmer mixture further minute. Stir in parsley, mint and pepper.

Serves 4.

Tomato Sauces

Neapolitan

Recipe can be made a day ahead. Reheat just before serving. Suitable to freeze.

30g butter
1 tablespoon olive oil
2 x 400g cans tomatoes
½ teaspoon dried basil (or 1 teaspoon chopped fresh basil)
2 tablespoons chopped fresh parsely

Heat butter and oil in pan. Sieve undrained tomatoes into pan; discard seeds. Stir in basil, simmer, uncovered, about 30 minutes or until sauce is reduced by about half. Stir in parsley just before serving.

Pizzaiola

Recipe can be made a day ahead. Reheat just before serving. Suitable to freeze.

1 tablespoon olive oil
1 large clove garlic
2 x 400g cans tomatoes
¼ teaspoon marjoram
2 tablespoons chopped fresh parsley

Heat oil in pan, add garlic, cook, stirring, until lightly browned; discard garlic. Sieve undrained tomatoes into frying pan; discard seeds. Stir in marjoram, simmer, uncovered, 30 minutes or until sauce is reduced by about half. Stir in parsley just before serving.

Serves 2.

Tuna & Mushroom

Recipe best made just before serving. Not suitable to freeze.

90g butter
1 large onion, finely chopped
450g can tuna, drained, flaked
90g button mushrooms, halved
300ml carton cream
2 tablespoons tomato paste
pinch ground black pepper
1 tablespoon chopped
   fresh parsley

Melt butter in pan, add onion and tuna, cook, stirring, until onion is soft. Add mushrooms, cream, paste and pepper, bring to boil, remove from heat immediately; stir in parsley.

Serves 4.

Oil & Garlic

Recipe best made just before serving. Not suitable to freeze.

**⅓ cup olive oil
3 cloves garlic, crushed
2 tablespoons chopped
   fresh parsley
ground black pepper**

Heat oil in pan, add garlic, cook gently until lightly browned. Stir in chopped parsley and pepper.
Serves 4.

Summer

Recipe best made a day ahead. Use only ripe tomatoes in season for the best flavor. Bring mixture to room temperature before serving. Not suitable to freeze.

500g firm, ripe tomatoes, finely chopped
1 onion, chopped
6 seedless green olives, finely chopped
1 tablepoon capers, finely chopped
2 cloves garlic, crushed
¼ teaspoon dried oregano leaves
⅓ cup chopped fresh parsley
½ cup olive oil

Combine all ingredients in bowl; mix well. Cover, refrigerate overnight. Toss through hot pasta before serving.

Serves 4.

Matriciana

Recipe can be made a day ahead. Reheat just before serving. Not suitable to freeze.

6 rashers lean bacon
1½ tablespoons olive oil
1 onion, finely chopped
500g ripe tomatoes, peeled, seeded, chopped
1 red chilli, seeded, finely chopped

Remove rind from bacon, cut bacon crossways into thin strips. Heat oil in pan, add bacon and onion, cook, stirring, until onion is soft; drain away excess fat. Add tomatoes and chilli; mix well. Simmer gently, uncovered, 5 minutes, stirring mixture occasionally.

Serves 4.

MINI CLASSICS

Alfredo

Recipe best made just before serving. Not suitable to freeze.

90g butter
⅔ cup cream
1 cup grated parmesan cheese
chopped fresh parsley

Combine butter and cream in pan, stir over low heat until butter is melted and well combined with cream. Remove from heat. Add cheese, stir until sauce is blended and smooth. Serve sprinkled with parsley.
Serves 4.

Carbonara

Recipe best made just before serving. Not suitable to freeze.

4 rashers bacon or pancetta
1/3 cup cream
pinch paprika
1 egg
1 egg yolk, extra
60g grated parmesan cheese
250g fettuccine or tagliatelle
30g butter
ground black pepper

Remove rind from bacon, cut bacon into thin strips. Gently cook bacon in pan until crisp. Drain all but 2 tablespoons of fat from pan. Add cream and paprika, stir until combined.

Beat egg, extra egg yolk and half the cheese in bowl until combined. Add fettuccine to large pan of boiling water, boil, uncovered, until just tender. Drain, return fettuccine to pan with butter, toss over low heat until combined.

Add bacon mixture, toss well. Add egg mixture, toss until combined. Season with pepper. Serve sprinkled with remaining parmesan cheese.

Serves 4 to 6.

Puttanesca

Recipe best made just before serving. Not suitable to freeze.

**4 ripe tomatoes
12 stuffed olives
45g can anchovy fillets
¼ cup olive oil
2 cloves garlic, crushed
1 tablespoon chopped fresh basil
pinch chilli powder
½ cup chopped fresh parsley**

Peel and chop tomatoes; slice olives. Drain and chop anchovies. Heat oil in pan, add garlic, cook, stirring, until garlic just changes colour. Add tomatoes, olives, anchovies, basil, chilli powder and parsley, cook, stirring, 3 minutes.

Serves 4.

Bolognaise

Recipe can be made 3 days ahead. Reheat just before serving. Suitable to freeze. A traditional bolognese sauce does not contain garlic, however, 2 crushed cloves of garlic can be added with the onion, if desired.

2 tablespoons olive oil
1 large onion, finely chopped
750g minced beef
400g can peeled tomatoes
⅓ cup tomato paste
1 teaspoon dried basil leaves
1 teaspoon dried oregano leaves
½ teaspoon dried thyme leaves
1 litre (4 cups) water
pinch ground black pepper
grated parmesan cheese

Heat oil in pan. Add onion, cook, stirring, until lightly browned. Add beef, cook, stirring, until well browned, mashing to break any lumps. Drain away excess fat.

Sieve undrained tomatoes into frying pan; discard seeds. Add paste, herbs, water and pepper; mix well.

Simmer very gently, uncovered, about 1¾ hours or until nearly all the liquid has evaporated. Serve topped with parmesan cheese.

Serves 4 to 6.

Chilli

Recipe best made just before serving. Not suitable to freeze.

250g spaghetti
125g butter
4 green shallots, finely chopped
3 red chillies, seeded, finely chopped
2 cloves garlic, crushed
2 tablespoons chopped fresh parsley

Add spaghetti to large pan of boiling water, boil, uncovered, until just tender; drain well. Heat butter in pan, add shallots, chillies and garlic, cook, stirring, 2 minutes. Add spaghetti and parsley, stir to combine. Serve topped with grated parmesan cheese, if desired.

Serves 2.

ITALIAN COOKING CLASS COOKBOOK

PASTA & RICE

Rice and pasta are popular throughout Italy. Sample the best of both with these recipes.

Risotto Milanese

Recipe best made just before serving. Not suitable to freeze.

60g butter
1 large onion, finely chopped
375g long grain rice
½ cup dry white wine
3 cups hot water
¼ teaspoon ground saffron
2 chicken stock cubes
30g butter, extra
2 tablespoons grated parmesan cheese

Heat butter in pan, add onion, cook, stirring, until soft. Add rice, stir until well coated with butter mixture. Add wine, 1 cup of the water, saffron and crumbled stock cubes. Boil, uncovered, until almost all the water has been absorbed, stirring occasionally. Add half the remaining hot water, stir well, boil, uncovered, until water has almost been absorbed, stirring occasionally. Stir in remaining hot water, simmer, uncovered, until water has been absorbed, stirring occasionally. Total cooking time for risotto is about 20 minutes. Stir in extra butter and cheese, stir gently until butter is just melted. Serves 6.

Suppli

Recipe can be prepared a day ahead. Deep-fry balls just before serving. Not suitable to freeze.

15g butter
1 small onion, chopped
1½ cups long grain rice
½ cup dry white wine
2½ cups hot water
pinch ground saffron
1 chicken stock cube
1 tablespoon (15g) butter, extra
1 tablespoon grated parmesan cheese
2 eggs, lightly beaten
80g mozzarella cheese
⅔ cup packaged dry breadcrumbs
oil for deep-frying

Heat butter in pan, add onion, cook, stirring, until soft. Add rice, cook, stirring, 2 minutes. Add wine, half the water, saffron and crumbled stock cube. Boil, uncovered, until water has almost been absorbed. Add remaining water, simmer, uncovered, about 12 minutes or until all water has been absorbed. Stir in extra butter and parmesan cheese; cool. Add eggs, stir gently, taking care not to mash the rice. Cut mozzarella into 1cm cubes.

Place a tablespoon of rice in one hand, add a cube of cheese, then cover cheese with another tablespoon of rice. Shape into a ball, completely enclosing cheese. Roll balls in breadcrumbs. Balls can be fried at once but are easier to handle if refrigerated a few hours. Deep-fry balls in batches in hot oil until they are golden brown; drain on absorbent paper. Serve while hot.
Makes about 18.

Rice & Peas

Recipe best made just before serving. Not suitable to freeze.

**60g butter
1 onion, finely chopped
1 stick celery, finely chopped
⅔ cup long grain rice
½ cup dry white wine
3 cups boiling water
2 chicken stock cubes
1kg fresh young peas, shelled
2 tablespoons grated parmesan cheese
30g butter, extra**

A specialty of Venice, this recipe is more moist than a risotto. It is sometimes classified as a soup but eaten, as any rice dish, with a fork.

Melt butter in pan, add onion and celery, cook, stirring, until lightly browned. Add rice, cook, stirring, about 3 minutes or until rice is covered with butter and becomes transparent. Add wine, 1 cup of the water and crumbled stock cubes; mix well. Bring to boil, stir in peas. Simmer, uncovered, until water has been absorbed.

Add half the remaining water, simmer, uncovered, until water has been absorbed. Add remaining water. Simmer, uncovered, until water is almost absorbed and peas are tender. Total cooking time should be about 20 minutes. Stir in cheese and extra butter.
Serves 4 to 6.

Vegetable Risotto

Recipe best made close to serving. Suitable to freeze.

**1 small eggplant
salt
60g butter
125g mushrooms
30g butter, extra
2 tablespoons olive oil
1 onion, chopped
500g long grain rice
1 litre (4 cups) hot water
2 chicken stock cubes
1 zucchini, thinly sliced
1/2 red pepper, chopped
1/2 green pepper, chopped
1 cup green peas
salt, pepper
1/2 cup grated parmesan cheese**

Cut eggplant into 1 cm slices, sprinkle with the salt, stand 1 hour.

Melt butter in pan, add mushrooms, cook, stirring, 2 minutes; remove from pan. Rinse eggplant, pat dry with absorbent paper, chop finely.

Heat extra butter and oil in pan, add onion and rice, cook, stirring, 2 minutes.

Add water and crumbled stock cubes to pan, simmer, covered, 15 minutes, stirring occasionally. Add mushrooms, zucchini, eggplant, peppers and peas; mix well. Simmer, uncovered, until all liquid has been absorbed and rice and vegetables tender. Add cheese, stir through gently. Press rice into lightly oiled bowl, turn onto plate.

Serves 6 to 8.

GNOCCHI & POLENTA

Gnocchi can be an entree or main course. Polenta is a traditional meal accompaniment.

Gnocchi alla Romana

Recipe can be prepared a day ahead. Bake just before serving. Not suitable to freeze.

3 cups milk
¼ teaspoon salt
pinch ground nutmeg
⅔ cup semolina
1 egg, lightly beaten
1½ cups grated parmesan cheese
60g butter, melted

Bring milk, salt and nutmeg to boil in pan. Reduce heat, gradually add semolina. Boil, stirring, about 10 minutes or until very thick. A wooden spoon should stand upright in centre of pan when mixture is ready. Remove from heat. Stir in combined egg and 1 cup of cheese; mix well.

Spread mixture into oiled oven tray, smoothing with wet spatula until 5mm thick. Cover, refrigerate about 1 hour or until firm. Turn firm semolina onto board, cut into 4cm rounds using a cutter. Arrange rounds in overlapping circles in shallow greased ovenproof dish, pour over butter, sprinkle with remaining cheese. Bake in moderate oven about 15 minutes or until crisp and lightly browned.
Serves 4 to 6.

Spinach gnocchi

Recipe can be prepared 3 hours ahead. Mould and cook gnocchi just before serving. Not suitable to freeze.

1 bunch (about 8 leaves) spinach
250g ricotta cheese
90g grated parmesan cheese
1 egg, lightly beaten
¼ teaspoon ground nutmeg
plain flour
45g butter, melted

Wash and dry spinach, remove stalks. Cook spinach leaves, without boiling, in large pan with tight-fitting lid until just tender. Drain well, chop finely. Combine spinach, ricotta cheese, half the parmesan cheese, egg and nutmeg in bowl; mix well.

Mould a rounded tablespoon of mixture into a ball or egg shape using a spoon and palm of hand; place onto tray covered with sifted flour. Repeat with remaining mixture.

Roll gnocchi in flour. Gradually add gnocchi to large pan of boiling water.

Simmer gently about 2 minutes or until gnocchi rise to surface. Remove from pan with slotted spoon.

Arrange gnocchi in well greased ovenproof dish in single layer. Pour over butter, sprinkle with remaining parmesan cheese. Cook under hot grill until cheese is lightly browned.

Serves 4 to 6 as an appetiser.

Polenta

Recipe can be prepared a day ahead. Cut and fry just before serving. Not suitable to freeze. Chicken or vegetable stock can be added to the water for extra flavour, if desired.

2 litres (8 cups) water
¼ teaspoon salt
2 cups cornmeal
¼ cup olive oil

Served plain, polenta is generally accompanied by a ragout such as bolognese sauce; or firm, it can be fried and served as an accompaniment to any meat. Hot, fried polenta also can be topped with anchovies and olives or other toppings and served as crostini.

Bring water and salt to boil in large pan. Gradually sprinkle cornmeal over water, stirring constantly to prevent lumps forming. Reduce heat to low. Simmer about 30 minutes or until polenta is very thick, stirring often. A wooden spoon should stand upright in centre of pan when mixture is ready. Spread mixture evenly into an oiled shallow 28cm x 18cm lamington tin. Cool, stand at room temperature about 3 hours or until firm.

Turn polenta onto board. Cut into 4cm slices or squares. Heat oil in pan until very hot, add polenta slices, cook gently 5 minutes or until polenta is golden brown on both sides.

Serves 4 to 6.

MINI CLASSICS

FISH & SHELLFISH

Perhaps it is with fish and shellfish that Italian cooking is at its subtle, most flavoursome best.

Fish Milanese

Fish can be crumbed a day ahead. Cook just before serving. Not suitable to freeze.

4 fish fillets
1 small onion, finely chopped
2 tablespoons lemon juice
⅓ cup olive oil
plain flour
2 eggs, lightly beaten
1 tablespoon milk
packaged dry breadcrumbs
1 tablespoon olive oil, extra
60g butter
60g butter, extra
1 clove garlic, crushed
2 teaspoons chopped fresh parsley

Remove skin from fish, remove bones. Combine onion, juice and oil in large dish; mix well. Add fish, spoon oil mixture over fish to coat thoroughly, cover, refrigerate 1 hour, turning occasionally.

Remove fish from marinade, coat lightly in flour, dip in combined eggs and milk, then into breadcrumbs, pressing crumbs on firmly.

Heat extra oil and butter in large pan. Add fish, cook until golden brown on both sides, turning once; drain on absorbent paper. Melt extra butter in separate pan, add garlic, cook, stirring, until butter is light golden brown; add parsley. Pour browned butter over fish.

Serves 4.

Marinated Calamari

Recipe best made a day ahead. Not suitable to freeze.

**500g squid
1/3 cup lemon juice
1/3 cup olive oil
1 clove garlic, crushed
1 tablespoon chopped fresh parsley**

Holding squid with one hand, gently pull head and entrails away in one piece. Cut tentacles from head. Remove bone found at open end of squid (it looks like a long, thin piece of plastic). Clean squid under cold running water, then peel away brown outer skin.

Cut squid evenly into 5mm rings. Drop rings into boiling water, simmer about 15 minutes or until tender; drain. Combine squid and remaining ingredients in bowl, cover, refrigerate overnight. Serve with marinade.

Calamari

Squid can be crumbed a day ahead. Cook just before serving. Not suitable to freeze.

1kg squid
1 egg, lightly beaten
2 tablespoons milk
2 cups packaged dry breadcrumbs
oil for deep or shallow frying

Clean squid. Cut squid into 5mm rings.

Dip squid rings into combined egg and milk, drain away excess. Toss squid in breadcrumbs, patting breadcrumbs on firmly to coat.

Deep-fry squid in batches in hot oil golden brown; drain on absorbent paper.

Alternatively, shallow-fry squid in batches in hot oil until golden brown, turning squid once during cooking; drain on absorbent paper. Serve hot with lemon wedges.

Serves 4.

MEAT & POULTRY

Veal teamed with luscious sauces is a favourite in Italy, and we've added other popular dishes too.

Chicken Cacciatore

Recipe can be made a day ahead. Reheat just before serving. Suitable to freeze.

1.5kg chicken (or chicken pieces)
2 tablespoons olive oil
1 onion, finely chopped
1 clove garlic, crushed
½ cup dry white wine
1½ tablespoons vinegar
1 chicken stock cube
½ cup water
400g can peeled tomatoes
1 teaspoon dried basil leaves
1 teaspoon sugar
3 anchovy fillets
¼ cup milk
¼ cup seedless black olives, halved
1 tablespoon chopped fresh parsley

Cut chicken into serving-sized pieces. Heat oil in pan, add chicken, cook until well browned. Place chicken in ovenproof dish. Drain all but 1 tablespoon juices from pan. Add onion and garlic, cook, stirring, until onion is soft. Add wine and vinegar, boil, uncovered, until reduced by half. Add crumbled stock cube and water, stir over high heat 2 minutes.

Sieve undrained tomatoes into bowl; discard seeds. Add tomatoes, basil and sugar to pan, simmer, uncovered, 1 minute. Pour tomato mixture over chicken, bake, covered, in moderate oven 1 hour.

Combine anchovies and milk in bowl, stand 5 minutes, drain; chop finely. Arrange chicken in serving dish; keep warm. Pour liquid into pan, boil, uncovered, 1 minute. Add anchovies, olives and parsley, simmer 2 minutes; pour over chicken.

Serves 4.

Osso Bucco

Recipe can be made a day ahead. Reheat just before serving. Suitable to freeze.

90g butter
2 carrots, chopped
2 large onions, finely chopped
3 sticks celery, finely chopped
1 clove garlic, crushed
4 veal shanks or knuckles, cut into 6cm pieces
plain flour
2 tablespoons olive oil
½ cup dry red wine
430g can beef consomme
1 teaspoon dried basil leaves
1 teaspoon dried thyme leaves
1 bay leaf
3cm strip lemon rind
2 x 400g cans whole tomatoes
GREMOLADA
1 clove garlic, crushed
¼ cup chopped fresh parsley
1 teaspoon grated lemon rind

Heat one-third of the butter in pan. Add carrots, onions, celery and half the garlic. Cook, stirring, until onions are golden brown. Remove from heat. Transfer vegetables to a large ovenproof dish.

Toss shanks in flour. Heat remaining butter and oil in large pan, add shanks, cook until well browned all over. Drain fat from pan. Add wine, consomme, herbs and lemon rind to pan. Sieve undrained tomatoes into pan; discard seeds. Stir over heat until boiling.

Carefully pack shanks upright on top of vegetables in dish. Pour sauce over shanks, bake, covered, in moderate oven about 1½ hours or until veal is very tender, stirring occasionally. Serve osso buco sprinkled with gremolada.

Gremolada: Combine garlic, parsley and rind in bowl.

Serves 6.

Veal Campagnola

Sauce can be made 2 days ahead. Recipe best made just before serving. Sauce suitable to freeze.

5 spinach leaves, shredded
30g butter
4 veal steaks
plain flour
30g butter, extra
1 tablespoon olive oil
4 slices mozzarella or gruyere cheese

TOMATO SAUCE
30g butter
2 cloves garlic, crushed
400g can whole tomatoes
1 tablespoon tomato paste
¼ cup dry white wine
¼ cup water
1 teaspoon sugar

Place spinach in pan with enough water to cover bottom of pan. Simmer, covered, until tender; drain well. Toss with butter. Trim veal, pound gently with meat mallet until thin. Toss steaks in flour, shake away excess flour.

Heat extra butter and oil in pan, add veal, cook, turning once, until almost cooked through; remove pan from heat. Divide spinach over veal, top with cheese. Pour tomato sauce around veal, taking care not to cover the cheese, cover, simmer gently about 10 minutes or until cheese is melted.

Tomato Sauce: Heat butter in pan, add garlic, cook 1 minute. Sieve undrained tomatoes into pan; discard seeds. Stir in paste, wine, water and sugar, simmer, uncovered, 5 minutes.

Serves 4.

Veal Scallops

Recipe best made just before serving. Not suitable to freeze.

4 veal steaks
30g butter
1 small onion, finely chopped
¼ cup dry sherry
2 teaspoons plain flour
½ cup water
½ beef stock cube
125g mushrooms, sliced
2 tablespoons cream

Remove any fat from veal, gently pound veal with meat mallet until thin. Melt butter in pan, add veal, cook, turning once, until well browned; remove from pan. Add onion to pan, cook, stirring, 2 minutes; stir in sherry. Bring to boil, boil, uncovered, 15 seconds. Remove from heat, stir in blended flour, water and crumbled stock cube. Stir over heat until mixture boils.

Return veal to pan, add mushrooms, simmer gently, covered, 8 minutes. Stir in cream, stir until heated through.
Serves 4.

Liver with Onions

Recipe best made just before serving. Not suitable to freeze.

500g calves liver (or lambs fry)
plain flour
30g butter
1 tablespoon olive oil
3 onions, thinly sliced
2 tablespoons olive oil, extra
1 tablespoon chopped fresh parsley
ground black pepper

Remove thin skin from around liver, cut liver evenly into thin strips. Toss liver in flour, place in sieve; shake away excess flour. Heat butter and oil pan, add onions, cook, stirring, until soft; remove from pan.

Heat extra oil in skillet, add liver, cook, stirring, about 2 minutes or until liver changes colour. Return onions to pan with parsley and pepper, cook, stirring, 2 minutes.

Serves 4.

Veal Casserole

Recipe can be made a day ahead. Reheat just before serving. Not suitable to freeze. Pancetta is a specially cured bacon, available from most delicatessens. If unavailable, substitute ham.

8 veal chops
60g butter
2 onions, quartered
3 cloves garlic, crushed
1 bulb fennel, sliced
125g pancetta, chopped
60g mushrooms, sliced
¾ cup dry white wine
1 cup water
1 chicken stock cube
1 tablespoon tomato paste
2 tablespoons plain flour
2 tablespoons water, extra

Remove any fat and gristle from chops. Melt butter in pan, add chops, cook until well browned on both sides. Place chops in ovenproof dish in single layer. Add onions, garlic, fennel, pancetta and mushrooms to pan, cook, stirring, 2 minutes. Add wine, water, crumbled stock cube and paste, bring to boil.

Pour vegetable mixture over chops, bake, covered, in moderate oven about 45 minutes or until chops are tender. Remove chops from dish; keep warm. Pour sauce and vegetables into pan, stir in blended flour and extra water. Stir over heat until mixture boils and thickens, pour over chops.

Serves 4.

SALADS & VEGETABLES

Colourful salads and vegetables provide variety. Try them as an entree or a light main course.

Radicchio & Fennel Salad

Recipe can be prepared 6 hours ahead. Not suitable to freeze.

1 radicchio lettuce
1 fennel bulb
30g black olives
DRESSING
¼ cup olive oil
1 tablespoon lemon juice
1 canned anchovy fillet
3 black seedless olives
pinch sugar

Separate and wash lettuce leaves. Cut fennel bulb in half, then into 1cm strips. Arrange lettuce, fennel strips and olives on serving plate. Spoon dressing over salad just before serving.
Dressing: Blend or process oil, juice, anchovy, olives and sugar until smooth.
Serves 2.

Calamari & Vegetables

Recipe best made just before serving. Not suitable to freeze.

45g can anchovy fillets, drained
3 cloves garlic
1 teaspoon chopped fresh parsley
1 tablespoon olive oil
4 small cleaned squid
1 egg, lightly beaten
1 cup dry packaged breadcrumbs
oil for deep-frying
1 small cucumber, thinly sliced
3 ripe tomatoes, quartered
2 teaspoons finely chopped fresh basil
1 green pepper, thinly sliced
1 avocado, chopped
¼ cup black olives
2 teaspoons dried oregano leaves
2 tablespoons olive oil, extra
1 tablespoon white wine vinegar
ground black pepper
4 large lettuce leaves

Place anchovies in small bowl. Add 1 clove crushed garlic, parsley and oil, stand while preparing salad.

Cut squid into thin rings. Dip squid into egg, then in bread-crumbs to coat. Deep-fry squid in batches in hot oil until golden brown; drain on absorbent paper.

Combine cucumber, remaining crushed garlic, tomatoes, basil, pepper, avocado, olives and oregano in bowl. Combine extra oil, vinegar and black pepper in jar; shake well. Add to salad, toss gently. Tear lettuce into pieces, place in serving bowl, top with salad. Arrange squid around edge of salad, arrange anchovies in centre of salad, spoon over anchovy marinade.
Serves 4 to 6.

Vegetable Salad

Recipe can be prepared 6 hours ahead. Not suitable to freeze.

2 ripe tomatoes, quartered
60g green olives
60g black olives
2 witlof
1 lettuce
1 bunch curly endive
DRESSING
¼ cup white vinegar
½ cup olive oil
1½ tablespoons chopped fresh basil
ground black pepper
pinch sugar

Combine tomatoes and olives in bowl, pour over dressing, mix lightly; stand 30 minutes.

Separate witlof leaves. Arrange witlof, lettuce and curly endive on large platter. Place tomatoes and olives in centre. Spoon dressing over top of salad just before serving.

Dressing: Whisk all ingredients together in bowl.

Serves 6.

Bagna Cauda

Recipe best made just before serving. Not suitable to freeze. Serve with crisp, chopped vegetables.

2 x 300ml cartons thickened cream
60g butter
2 cloves garlic, crushed
45g can anchovy fillets, drained, finely chopped

Place cream in pan, bring to boil, simmer, uncovered, about 15 minutes or until cream is thickened, stirring frequently.

Melt butter in separate pan over low heat, taking care not to brown butter. Add garlic and anchovies, stir until mixture is well blended and is a paste consistency. Stir in hot cream; mix well. Serve warm.

Serves 6.

Cauliflower Neapolitan

Recipe can be made a day ahead. Not suitable to freeze.

**8 stuffed green olives
½ cauliflower
½ small onion, finely sliced
1 small stick celery, chopped
½ cup olive oil
2 tablespoons lemon juice
4 capers
2 tablespoons chopped
   fresh parsley
ground black pepper**

If desired, remove centres from olives, cut olives into thin slices. Cut cauliflower into small flowerets, add to pan of boiling water, boil 5 minutes; drain. Place into bowl of cold water, stand 30 minutes; drain well.

Combine olives, onion, celery, oil, juice, capers, parsley and pepper in large bowl. Add cauliflower; toss well. Serves 4.

MINI CLASSICS

Tomato & Salami

Recipe best prepared several hours ahead. Not suitable to freeze.

125g sliced salami
⅓ cup olive oil
1 tablespoon lemon juice
½ teaspoon grated lemon rind
ground black pepper
1 clove garlic, crushed
1 tablespoon chopped fresh parsley
1 tablespoon chopped fresh basil
4 ripe tomatoes

Place salami in shallow dish. Pour over combined oil, juice, rind, pepper, garlic, parsley and basil; stand 1 hour, turning once.

Cut tomatoes into thick slices. Arrange overlapping slices of tomato and salami on serving plate, pour over remaining oil mixture before serving.

Serves 4 to 6.

ITALIAN COOKING CLASS COOKBOOK

SWEET TREATS

In Italy, desserts are prepared for special occasions but these treats are great any time.

Coconut Biscuits

Recipe can be made a week ahead. Suitable to freeze.

2 large egg yolks
¼ cup caster sugar
2 cups shredded coconut
1 large egg white

Beat egg yolks and sugar in bowl with electric mixer until creamy, stir in coconut. Beat egg white in separate bowl until firm peaks form, gently fold into coconut mixture.

Drop teaspoons of mixture onto greased oven trays. Bake in slow oven 15 minutes, reduce heat to very slow, bake further 30 minutes or until biscuits are golden brown.

Makes about 18.

Fig & Nut Cake

Recipe can be made 2 days ahead. Suitable to freeze.

3 eggs
½ cup caster sugar
90g dark chocolate, finely chopped
90g slivered almonds, chopped
125g dried figs, chopped
125g mixed peel, chopped
125g roasted hazelnuts, chopped
1¼ cups self-raising flour

Grease a 20cm x 10cm loaf pan, line base with paper, grease paper.

Beat eggs and sugar in small bowl with electric mixer until pale and fluffy. Fold in choolate, nuts, figs and peel. Gently fold in sifted flour. Spread mixture into prepared pan. Bake in moderate oven about 1 hour or until light golden brown and cooked when tested. Cool slightly in pan, turn onto wire rack to cool completely.

Almond Biscuits

Recipe can be made 1 week ahead. Suitable to freeze.

1 egg white
¼ cup caster sugar
1 tablespoon honey
1 teaspoon grated lemon rind
2 cups ground almonds
1 tablespoon self-raising flour
1 egg white, lightly beaten, extra
TOPPING
½ cup caster sugar
¼ teaspoon vanilla essence

Beat egg white in small bowl until soft peaks form, gradually add sugar and honey, beat until sugar is dissolved between additions. Add rind, almonds and sifted flour; mix well. Shape tablespoons of mixture into 5cm lengths, place onto greased oven trays. Bake in moderately slow oven about 40 minutes or until lightly browned.

Reserve 2 teaspoons of extra egg white for topping. Brush tops of cookies with remaining egg white. Press a teaspoon of topping onto warm cookies with a spoon. The topping will harden on cooling. Store in airtight container.
Topping: Combine reserved egg white, sugar and essence in bowl.
Makes about 16.

Sicilian Creams

Biscuits can be made a day ahead. Cut and fill close to serving. Unfilled cookies suitable to freeze. Any liqueur can be used, e.g. Galliano, Grand Marnier, Cointreau, Amaretto.

**1¾ cups self-raising flour
60g butter
½ cup caster sugar
1 teaspoon grated lemon rind
1 teaspoon vanilla essence
1 egg, lightly beaten
¼ cup milk
1 tablespoon water
1 tablespoon liqueur
whipped cream
icing sugar mixture**

Sift flour into bowl, rub in butter, add caster sugar; mix well. Make well in centre, add combined rind, essence, egg and milk, mix with wooden spoon to a soft, pliable dough.

Turn dough onto lightly floured surface, knead gently until smooth; dough should be soft and pliable. Roll dough out until 1cm thick, cut into 5cm rounds using cutter. Place rounds on lightly greased oven trays, about 3cm apart. Bake in moderate oven about 15 minutes or until lightly browned; cool on wire rack.

Cut cold biscuits in half using a fine serrated knife, brush underside of tops with combined water and liqueur. Sandwich biscuits with whipped cream, dust with sifted icing sugar.

Makes about 12.

Apple Cream Pie

Recipe can be made a day ahead. Not suitable to freeze.

1¼ cups plain flour
½ teaspoon ground cinnamon
1 teaspoon baking powder
¼ cup caster sugar
2 teaspoons grated lemon rind
125g butter
1 egg yolk, lightly beaten
2 tablespoons dry sherry
2 green apples, peeled
1 teaspoon ground cinnamon, extra
300ml carton cream

FILLING
2 eggs
½ cup sugar
2 tablespoons plain flour
2 teaspoons grated lemon rind
½ cup cream
250g cream cheese, softened
1 tablespoon mixed peel
¼ cup chopped raisins

Sift dry ingredients into bowl, add rind, rub in butter. Add combined egg yolk and sherry, mix to a firm dough, press mixture into a ball.

Roll out pastry until large enough to line shallow 28cm x 18cm lamington pan, lift into pan; trim edges.

Quarter cored apples, slice thinly. Arrange slices in slightly overlapping rows in pastry base. Pour filling over apples. Bake in moderate oven 1¼ hours. To serve warm, sprinkle with extra cinnamon, serve with cream. To serve cold, stand until cold, spread with cream, sprinkle with extra cinnamon.

Filling: Beat eggs and sugar in bowl until thick, gradually add sifted flour, rind, cream, cream cheese, peel and raisins; mix well.

Serves 6.

Sicilian Cheesecake

Recipe can be made 2 days ahead. Not suitable to freeze. Any mixture of glace fruits can be used in this recipe.

185g plain chocolate biscuits, crushed
90g butter, melted
½ cup cream, whipped
60g dark chocolate, grated
FILLING
625g ricotta cheese
1 cup icing sugar mixture
1 teaspoon vanilla essence
2 tablespoons Creme de Cacao liqueur
60g dark chocolate
2 tablespoons chopped glace fruit

Combine biscuits and butter in bowl; mix well. Press mixture evenly over base of 20cm springform pan. Refrigerate while preparing filling. Spoon filling into pan, spread evenly, refrigerate 6 hours or overnight. Spread cream over top of cake, sprinkle edge with chocolate.

Filling: Combine cheese, sifted sugar, essence and liqueur in small bowl, beat until smooth and fluffy. Grate chocolate, stir into cheese mixture with glace fruit; mix well.

Glazed Oranges

*Recipe can be made 2 days ahead. Not suitable to freeze.
It is important to remove white pith from oranges as it is quite bitter and will adversely affect the taste.*

4 oranges
1¼ cups sugar
1½ cups water
¼ cup water, extra
2 tablespoons Grand Marnier liqueur
2 teaspoons lemon juice

Using a vegetable peeler, cut strips of peel thinly from 2 oranges. Remove any white pith from strips. Cut into thin strips. Peel all oranges, removing white pith. Cut oranges horizontally into 4 slices for easy serving. Reassemble oranges, secure with wooden skewers.

Place peel strips in pan, cover with water, boil, uncovered, 10 minutes; drain. Combine sugar and water in pan, stir over heat until sugar is dissolved; add peel strips. Boil gently, uncovered, about 10 minutes or until strips are transparent and glazed. Remove strips from syrup, place on oiled plate.

Boil syrup, uncovered, further 5 minutes or until syrup turns pale golden brown. Remove from heat, quickly add extra water (mixture will crackle), stir to dissolve any toffee in base of pan. Stand 5 minutes, stir in liqueur and juice; cool. Pour syrup over oranges, add glazed peel strips, cover; refrigerate several hours or overnight. Remove skewers from glazed oranges just before serving. Serve oranges topped with peel strips and drizzled with syrup.

Serves 4.

Zabaglione

Recipe best made just before serving. Not suitable to freeze. Any favorite liqueur can be used. Zabaglione makes an excellent topping for fresh fruit, and is also delicious served warm over ice cream.

5 egg yolks
¼ cup caster sugar
½ cup marsala
¼ cup dry white wine

Combine egg yolks and sugar in top half of double saucepan. Beat with hand beater or electric mixer until well combined. Place over simmering water. Gradually beat in half the marsala and half the white wine; beat well. Gradually beat in remaining marsala and wine. Beat constantly about 10 minutes or until thick and creamy. If mixture adheres to side of pan, quickly remove from simmering water, beat vigorously with wooden spoon – especially around base of pan. Pour into individual dishes.

Serves 4.

Almond Crunch

Recipe can be made 1 week ahead. Not suitable to freeze. For best results, use a sweets thermometer.

1¾ cups sugar
2 tablespoons lemon juice
155g (1 cup) whole blanched almonds
¼ cup golden syrup
300ml carton cream

Lightly oil a marble slab or dish that has been sprinkled with water. Combine ½ cup of the sugar and all the juice in large pan. Stir over heat until sugar is dissolved. Boil, without stirring, about 6 minutes or until mixture turns dark golden brown. Remove from heat, add almonds; mix well. Drop mixture onto prepared marble slab; cool.

Oil a shallow 28cm x 18cm lamington pan. Place remaining sugar, golden syrup and cream in large heavy saucepan, stir over heat until sugar is dissolved. Stir until mixture comes to the boil, boil, without stirring, until a teaspoon of mixture dropped into a cup of cold water forms a hard ball between the fingers (126°F on sweets thermometer). This will take about 30 minutes. Do not allow mixture to boil over. While mixture is boiling, break almond toffee into pieces, blend or process until fine.

Quickly stir processed almond toffee into cream mixture, pour into prepared pan; cool slightly. Using knife, mark into 2.5cm squares; stand until cold. Cut into squares when cold.

QUICK CONVERSION GUIDE

Wherever you live in the world you can use our recipes with the help of our easy-to-follow conversions for all your cooking needs. These conversions are approximate only. The difference between the exact and approximate conversions of liquid and dry measures amounts to only a teaspoon or two, and will not make any difference to your cooking results.

MEASURING EQUIPMENT

The difference between measuring cups internationally is minimal within 2 or 3 teaspoons' difference. (For the record, 1 Australian metric measuring cup will hold approximately 250ml.) The most accurate way of measuring dry ingredients is to weigh them. When measuring liquids use a clear glass or plastic jug with metric markings.
In this book we use metric measuring cups and spoons approved by Standards Australia.

- a graduated set of four cups for measuring dry ingredients; the sizes are marked on the cups.
- a graduated set of four spoons for measuring dry and liquid ingredients; the amounts are marked on the spoons.
- 1 TEASPOON: 5ml.
- 1 TABLESPOON: 20ml.

NOTE: NZ, CANADA, USA AND UK ALL USE 15ml TABLESPOONS.
ALL CUP AND SPOON MEASUREMENTS ARE LEVEL.

DRY MEASURES

METRIC	IMPERIAL
15g	½oz
30g	1oz
60g	2oz
90g	3oz
125g	4oz (¼lb)
155g	5oz
185g	6oz
220g	7oz
250g	8oz (½lb)
280g	9oz
315g	10oz
345g	11oz
375g	12oz (¾lb)
410g	13oz
440g	14oz
470g	15oz
500g	16oz (1lb)
750g	24oz (1½lb)
1kg	32oz (2lb)

LIQUID MEASURES

METRIC	IMPERIAL
30ml	1 fluid oz
60ml	2 fluid oz
100ml	3 fluid oz
125ml	4 fluid oz
150ml	5 fluid oz (¼ pint/1 gill)
190ml	6 fluid oz
250ml	8 fluid oz
300ml	10 fluid oz (½ pint)
500ml	16 fluid oz
600ml	20 fluid oz (1 pint)
1000ml (1 litre)	1¾ pints

WE USE LARGE EGGS WITH AN AVERAGE WEIGHT OF 60G.

HELPFUL MEASURES

METRIC	IMPERIAL
3mm	⅛in
6mm	¼in
1cm	½in
2cm	¾in
2.5cm	1in
5cm	2in
6cm	2½in
8cm	3in
10cm	4in
13cm	5in
15cm	6in
18cm	7in
20cm	8in
23cm	9in
25cm	10in
28cm	11in
30cm	12in (1ft)

HOW TO MEASURE

When using the graduated metric measuring cups, it is important to shake the dry ingredients loosely into the required cup. Do not tap the cup on the bench, or pack the ingredients into the cup unless otherwise directed. Level top of cup with knife. When using graduated metric measuring spoons, level top of spoon with knife. When measuring liquids in the jug, place jug on flat surface, check for accuracy at eye level.

OVEN TEMPERATURES

These oven temperatures are only a guide; we've given you the lower degree of heat. Always check the manufacturer's manual.

	C˚ (Celsius)	F˚ (Fahrenheit)	Gas Mark
Very slow	120	250	1
Slow	150	300	2
Moderately slow	160	325	3
Moderate	180 – 190	350 – 375	4
Moderately hot	200 – 210	400 – 425	5